D0529811

DUMP
CASSEROLES

DELICIOUS COMFORT FOOD MADE EASY

Publications International, Ltd.

Copyright © 2016 Publications International, Ltd.
All rights reserved. This publication may not be reproduced or quoted in whole or in part by any means whatsoever without written permission from:

Louis Weber, CEO
Publications International, Ltd.
8140 Lehigh Avenue
Morton Grove, IL 60053

Permission is never granted for commercial purposes.

Favorite Brand Name Recipes is a trademark of Publications International, Ltd.

All recipes that contain specific brand names are copyrighted by those companies, unless otherwise specified. All other recipes and all photographs *except* those on pages 5, 43, 61, 67, 73, 77, 83, 105, 111, 113 and 121 copyright © Publications International, Ltd.

Campbell's® and Prego® registered trademarks of CSC Brands LP. All rights reserved.

Pepperidge Farm® registered trademark of Pepperidge Farm, Incorporated. All rights reserved.

Pictured on the front cover: Sausage, Beef & Bean Casserole *(page 42)*.

Pictured on the back cover *(left to right):* Creamy Chicken Florentine *(page 76)*, Shrimp Creole *(page 94)* and It's a Keeper Casserole *(page 26)*.

ISBN: 978-1-68022-334-7

Library of Congress Control Number: 2016934621

Manufactured in China.

8 7 6 5 4 3 2 1

Microwave Cooking: Microwave ovens vary in wattage. Use the cooking times as guidelines and check for doneness before adding more time.

Preparation/Cooking Times: Preparation times are based on the approximate amount of time required to assemble the recipe before cooking, baking, chilling or serving. These times include preparation steps such as measuring, chopping and mixing. The fact that some preparations and cooking can be done simultaneously is taken into account. Preparation of optional ingredients and serving suggestions is not included.

TABLE OF CONTENTS

BEEF

Beef & Pasta Bake

Prep Time: 10 minutes ☰ Bake Time: 25 minutes ☰ Total Time: 35 minutes

- 1 **pound ground beef**
- 1 **jar (24 ounces) PREGO® Chunky Garden Mushroom Supreme Italian Sauce**
- 1 **cup shredded mozzarella cheese (about 4 ounces)**
- ½ **of a 16-ounce package medium tube-shaped pasta (ziti), cooked and drained (about 5 cups)**

1. Cook the beef in a 12-inch skillet over medium-high heat until well browned, stirring often to separate the meat. Pour off any fat.

2. Stir the Italian sauce and ½ **cup** cheese in the skillet. Add the pasta and stir to coat. Spoon the beef mixture into a 2-quart shallow baking dish.

3. Sprinkle with the remaining cheese.

4. Bake at 400°F. for 25 minutes or until hot and bubbling.

Makes 4 servings

QUICK BEEF STEW IN FOIL

- 1 sheet (20×12 inches) heavy-duty foil
- 8 ounces boneless beef top sirloin steak, cut into 1-inch pieces
- 1 medium red potato, peeled and cut into ¾-inch cubes
- 1 cup frozen mixed vegetables
- ⅔ cup beef gravy
- ½ teaspoon dried parsley flakes
- ¼ teaspoon salt
- ¼ teaspoon dried thyme
- ⅛ teaspoon black pepper

1. Preheat oven to 450°F. Spray foil with nonstick cooking spray.

2. Combine steak, potato, vegetables, gravy, parsley flakes, salt, thyme and pepper in medium bowl; mix well.

3. Spoon beef mixture into center of foil sheet. Double fold sides and ends of foil to seal packet, leaving head space for heat circulation. Place packet on baking sheet.

4. Bake 30 minutes or until beef is tender. Carefully open one end of packet to allow steam to escape.

Makes 2 servings

Rigatoni à la Vodka

- 12 ounces uncooked rigatoni pasta, cooked and drained
- 1 pound ground beef
- 1 jar (26 ounces) pasta sauce
- 1½ cups 3-cheese pasta sauce
- 4 cups (16 ounces) shredded mozzarella and Cheddar cheese blend, divided
- ¼ cup plus 2 tablespoons vodka

1. Preheat oven to 350°F. Spray 3-quart casserole with nonstick cooking spray. Place pasta in prepared casserole.

2. Brown beef in large skillet over medium heat 5 minutes, stirring to break up meat. Drain fat.

3. Add pasta sauces, 2 cups cheese and vodka to skillet; cook and stir until heated through. Add mixture to pasta; stir until well blended. Sprinkle with remaining 2 cups cheese.

4. Bake 15 minutes or until cheese is melted.

Makes 4 servings

Taco Salad Casserole

1 pound ground beef

1 cup chopped onion

1 can (15 ounces) chili with beans

1 can (about 14 ounces) diced tomatoes

1 can (4 ounces) diced green chiles, undrained

1 package (about 1 ounce) taco seasoning mix

1 bag (12 ounces) nacho-flavor tortilla chips, crushed

2 cups (8 ounces) shredded Cheddar cheese

2 cups (8 ounces) shredded mozzarella cheese

3 to 4 cups shredded lettuce

1 jar (8 ounces) prepared taco sauce

½ cup sour cream

1. Preheat oven to 350°F.

2. Brown beef and onion in large skillet over medium heat 6 to 8 minutes, stirring to break up meat. Drain fat.

3. Add chili with beans, tomatoes with juice, chiles and taco seasoning mix; cook and stir until heated through. Place half of crushed tortilla chips in 2½-quart casserole. Pour beef mixture over chips; top with Cheddar, mozzarella and remaining chips.

4. Bake 30 to 40 minutes or until hot and bubbly. Serve over lettuce; top with taco sauce and sour cream.

Makes 6 to 8 servings

Pizza Casserole

1½ pounds ground beef

1 medium onion, chopped

Salt and black pepper

2 cups uncooked rotini or other spiral pasta, cooked and drained

1 can (about 15 ounces) pizza sauce

1 can (8 ounces) tomato sauce

1 can (6 ounces) tomato paste

2 cups (8 ounces) shredded mozzarella cheese, divided

½ teaspoon garlic salt

½ teaspoon dried oregano

12 to 15 slices pepperoni

1. Preheat oven to 350°F.

2. Brown beef and onion in large ovenproof skillet over medium-high heat 6 to 8 minutes, stirring to break up meat. Drain fat. Season with salt and pepper.

3. Add pasta, pizza sauce, tomato sauce, tomato paste, 1 cup cheese, garlic salt and oregano; stir until blended. Sprinkle with remaining 1 cup cheese; top with pepperoni slices.

4. Bake 25 to 30 minutes or until cheese is melted and casserole is heated through.

Makes 6 servings

BISCUIT-TOPPED HEARTY STEAK PIE

1½ pounds boneless top round steak, cooked and cut into 1-inch pieces

1 package (9 ounces) frozen baby carrots

1 package (9 ounces) frozen peas and pearl onions

1 large baking potato, baked, peeled and cut into ½-inch pieces

1 jar (18 ounces) homestyle brown gravy

½ teaspoon dried thyme

½ teaspoon black pepper

1 can (10 ounces) refrigerated flaky buttermilk biscuits

1. Preheat oven to 375°F. Spray 2-quart baking dish with nonstick cooking spray.

2. Combine steak, carrots, peas and onions, potato, gravy, thyme and pepper in large bowl. Pour into prepared baking dish.

3. Bake 40 minutes. Remove from oven. *Increase oven temperature to 400°F.* Top with biscuits; bake 8 to 10 minutes or until biscuits are golden brown.

Makes 6 servings

VARIATIONS: This casserole can be prepared with leftovers of almost any kind. Other steaks, roast beef, stew meat, pork, lamb or chicken can be substituted for the round steak. Adjust the gravy flavor to complement the meat. Red potatoes can be used in place of the baking potato, and other frozen vegetable blends can be substituted for the carrots, peas and onions.

MEATBALL AND VEGETABLE CASSEROLE

6 potatoes, peeled and thinly sliced

6 to 8 carrots, thinly sliced

2 onions, thinly sliced

Salt and black pepper

1 can (46 ounces) tomato juice

1 can (10 ounces) diced tomatoes with green chiles

16 cooked meatballs

1. Preheat oven to 375°F. Spray 13×9-inch baking dish with nonstick cooking spray.

2. Place potatoes, carrots and onions in single overlapping layer in prepared baking dish. Season with salt and pepper. Combine tomato juice and tomatoes; pour over vegetables.

3. Bake 1½ hours or until vegetables are tender. Top with meatballs; bake 15 minutes or until browned.

Makes 8 servings

Farm-Style Casserole

  1 tablespoon canola oil
  1 small onion, chopped
  1 clove garlic, minced
  1 pound ground beef
  1 can (about 14 ounces) diced tomatoes
  1 cup frozen corn
  1 cup frozen baby lima beans
  1 teaspoon salt
  ½ teaspoon dried oregano
  ¼ teaspoon black pepper
  2 cups cooked macaroni or other pasta
  1 cup crushed tortilla chips

1. Preheat oven to 350°F.

2. Heat oil in large nonstick skillet over medium heat. Add onion and garlic; cook and stir 5 to 6 minutes or until onion is tender. Add beef; brown 6 to 8 minutes, stirring to break up meat. Drain fat.

3. Add tomatoes, corn, lima beans, salt, oregano and pepper; cook and stir over high heat 5 minutes or until all liquid is evaporated. Stir in macaroni. Transfer to 9-inch square baking dish; sprinkle with tortilla chips.

4. Bake 20 minutes or until heated through.

Makes 4 to 6 servings

Baked Ziti

PREP TIME: 20 minutes ☰ COOK TIME: 1 hour

REYNOLDS WRAP® Non-Stick Foil

1 pound ground beef, browned and drained

4 cups (32-ounce jar) chunky garden-style pasta sauce

1 tablespoon Italian seasoning, divided

1 package (16 ounces) ziti pasta, cooked and drained

1 package (8 ounces) shredded mozzarella cheese, divided

1 container (16 ounces) ricotta cheese or cottage cheese

1 egg

¼ cup grated Parmesan cheese, divided

1. Preheat oven to 350°F.

2. Combine ground beef, pasta sauce and 2 teaspoons Italian seasoning. Stir pasta into meat sauce; spread half of mixture evenly in pan. Top with half of mozzarella cheese.

3. Combine ricotta cheese, egg, 2 tablespoons Parmesan cheese and remaining Italian seasoning; spread over mozzarella cheese in pan. Spread remaining pasta mixture over ricotta cheese mixture. Sprinkle with remaining mozzarella and Parmesan cheeses.

4. Cover with REYNOLDS WRAP® Non-Stick Foil with non-stick (dull) side toward food.

5. Bake 45 minutes. Remove foil and continue baking 15 minutes or until cheese is melted and lightly browned. Let stand 15 minutes before serving.

Makes 8 servings

FAMILY-STYLE FRANKFURTERS WITH RICE AND BEANS

- 1 tablespoon vegetable oil
- 1 onion, chopped
- ½ green bell pepper, chopped
- 2 cloves garlic, minced
- 1 can (about 15 ounces) black beans, rinsed and drained
- 1 can (about 15 ounces) Great Northern beans, rinsed and drained
- 8 ounces beef frankfurters, cut into ¼-inch-thick slices
- 1 cup uncooked instant brown rice
- 1 cup vegetable broth
- ¼ cup packed brown sugar
- ¼ cup ketchup
- 3 tablespoons dark molasses
- 1 tablespoon Dijon mustard

1. Preheat oven to 350°F. Spray 13×9-inch baking dish with nonstick cooking spray.

2. Heat oil in large saucepan over medium-high heat. Add onion, bell pepper and garlic; cook and stir 2 minutes or until tender.

3. Add beans, frankfurters, rice, broth, brown sugar, ketchup, molasses and mustard to saucepan; gently stir until blended. Transfer to prepared baking dish.

4. Cover and bake 30 minutes or until rice is tender.

Makes 6 servings

CHILI SPAGHETTI BAKE

8 ounces uncooked spaghetti, cooked and drained

1 pound ground beef

1 medium onion, chopped

1 can (about 15 ounces) vegetarian chili with beans

1 can (about 14 ounces) Italian-style stewed tomatoes

1½ cups (6 ounces) shredded sharp Cheddar cheese, divided

½ cup sour cream

1½ teaspoons chili powder

¼ teaspoon garlic powder

¼ teaspoon salt

⅛ teaspoon black pepper

1. Preheat oven to 350°F. Spray 13×9-inch baking dish with nonstick cooking spray. Place spaghetti in prepared dish.

2. Brown beef and onion in large skillet over medium-high heat 6 to 8 minutes, stirring to break up meat. Drain fat.

3. Add chili, tomatoes, 1 cup cheese, sour cream, chili powder, garlic powder, salt and pepper to skillet; stir until well blended. Sprinkle with remaining ½ cup cheese.

4. Cover with foil and bake 30 minutes or until hot and bubbly. Let stand 5 minutes before serving.

Makes 8 servings

It's a Keeper Casserole

- 1 tablespoon vegetable oil
- ½ cup chopped onion
- ¼ cup chopped green bell pepper
- 1 clove garlic, minced
- 2 tablespoons all-purpose flour
- 1 teaspoon sugar
- ½ teaspoon salt
- ½ teaspoon dried basil
- ½ teaspoon black pepper
- 1 package (about 16 ounces) frozen meatballs, cooked
- 1 can (about 14 ounces) whole tomatoes, cut up and drained
- 1½ cups cooked vegetables (any combination)
- 1 teaspoon beef bouillon granules
- 1 teaspoon Worcestershire sauce
- 1 can (12 ounces) refrigerated buttermilk biscuits

1. Preheat oven to 400°F.

2. Heat oil in large saucepan over medium heat. Add onion, bell pepper and garlic; cook and stir until vegetables are tender. Stir in flour, sugar, salt, basil and black pepper until blended. Add meatballs, tomatoes, vegetables, bouillon and Worcestershire sauce; cook and stir until slightly thickened and bubbly. Transfer to 2-quart casserole; top with biscuits.

3. Bake 15 minutes or until biscuits are golden brown.

Makes 4 servings

Cajun-Style Beef and Beans

- 1 pound ground beef
- ¾ cup chopped onion
- 2½ cups cooked brown rice
- 1 can (about 15 ounces) kidney beans, rinsed and drained
- 1 can (about 14 ounces) stewed tomatoes
- 2 teaspoons Cajun seasoning, or to taste
- 1 cup (4 ounces) shredded Cheddar cheese

1. Preheat oven to 350°F.

2. Brown beef in large skillet over medium-high heat 6 to 8 minutes, stirring to break up meat. Drain fat. Add onion; cook and stir 3 minutes or until translucent.

3. Combine beef mixture, rice, beans, tomatoes and Cajun seasoning in 2- to 2½-quart casserole; mix well.

4. Cover and bake 25 to 30 minutes, stirring once. Sprinkle with cheese; cover and let stand 5 minutes before serving.

Makes 6 servings

PORK

BACON AND EGGS BRUNCH CASSEROLE

PREP TIME: 15 minutes ☰ COOK TIME: 35 minutes

- 1 tube (8 ounces) refrigerated crescent roll dough
- 6 eggs
- ½ cup milk
- 1 cup (4 ounces) SARGENTO® Traditional Cut Shredded Mild Cheddar Cheese
- 8 slices bacon, diced and cooked until crisp

SPRAY 13×9-inch baking pan with nonstick cooking spray. Unroll dough and press into bottom of pan. Bake in preheated 350°F oven 10 minutes.

BEAT together eggs and milk in medium bowl. Pour over partially baked dough. Sprinkle with cheese and bacon; return to oven and bake 25 minutes more or until center is set.

Makes 6 servings

Spanish Rice and Squash

    2 small yellow summer squash, cut into ¼-inch slices
    1 small zucchini, cut into ¼-inch slices
    1 package (about 12 ounces) Spanish rice mix
    2 cups water
    1 can (about 14 ounces) diced tomatoes
    1 can (about 4 ounces) sliced mushrooms, drained
    3 tablespoons butter, melted
    1 pound smoked sausage, cut into 4-inch pieces
    1 can (about 3 ounces) French fried onions
    1 cup (4 ounces) shredded mozzarella cheese

1. Preheat oven to 350°F. Spray 3-quart casserole with nonstick cooking spray. Place yellow squash and zucchini in prepared casserole.

2. Combine rice mix, water, tomatoes, mushrooms and butter in medium bowl; mix well. Pour over squash; top with sausage.

3. Cover and bake 20 minutes. Place fried onions around edge of casserole; sprinkle cheese in center. Bake, uncovered, 5 to 10 minutes or until cheese is melted.

Makes 4 to 6 servings

SAUSAGE PIZZA PIE CASSEROLE

- 8 ounces mild Italian sausage, casings removed
- 1 package (about 14 ounces) refrigerated pizza dough
- ½ cup tomato sauce
- 2 tablespoons chopped fresh basil *or* 2 teaspoons dried basil
- ½ teaspoon dried oregano
- ¼ teaspoon red pepper flakes
- 3 ounces mushrooms, quartered
- ½ cup thinly sliced red onion
- ½ cup thinly sliced green bell pepper
- ½ cup seeded diced tomato
- ½ cup sliced pitted black olives
- 8 slices smoked provolone cheese
- 2 tablespoons grated Parmesan and Romano cheese blend

1. Preheat oven to 350°F. Spray 13×9-inch baking dish with nonstick cooking spray.

2. Brown sausage in large nonstick skillet over medium-high heat 6 to 8 minutes, stirring to break up meat. Drain fat.

3. Unroll pizza dough in prepared baking dish; press evenly into bottom and up sides of dish. Spoon tomato sauce evenly over dough; sprinkle with basil, oregano and red pepper flakes. Layer with sausage, mushrooms, onion, bell pepper, tomato, olives and provolone cheese. Roll down sides of crust to form rim.

4. Bake 20 to 25 minutes or until crust is golden brown. Sprinkle with cheese blend; let stand 5 minutes before serving.

Makes 4 servings

HAM AND ASPARAGUS STRATA

PREP TIME: 15 minutes ☰ BAKE TIME: 45 minutes ☰ STAND TIME: 5 minutes

- **4** cups PEPPERIDGE FARM® Cubed Country Style Stuffing
- **2** cups shredded Swiss cheese (about 8 ounces)
- **1½** cups cooked cut asparagus
- **1½** cups cubed cooked ham
- **1** can (10¾ ounces) CAMPBELL'S® Condensed Cream of Asparagus Soup *or* Condensed Cream of Mushroom Soup
- **2** cups milk
- **5** eggs
- **1** tablespoon Dijon-style mustard

1. Heat the oven to 350°F. Stir the stuffing, cheese, asparagus and ham in a greased 3-quart shallow baking dish.

2. Beat the soup, milk, eggs and mustard in a medium bowl with a fork or whisk. Pour over the stuffing mixture. Stir and press the stuffing mixture into the milk mixture to coat.

3. Bake for 45 minutes or until a knife inserted in the center comes out clean. Let stand for 5 minutes.

Makes 8 servings

KITCHEN TIP: For **1½ cups** cooked cut asparagus, use **¾ pound** fresh asparagus, trimmed and cut into 1-inch pieces **or 1 package** frozen asparagus spears, thawed, drained and cut into 1-inch pieces.

Biscuit and Sausage Bake

- 2 cups biscuit baking mix
- ½ cup milk
- 1 egg
- 1 teaspoon vanilla
- 1 cup fresh or frozen blueberries
- 6 fully cooked breakfast sausage links, thawed if frozen, cut into small pieces
- Maple syrup

1. Preheat oven to 350°F. Spray 8-inch square baking pan with nonstick cooking spray.

2. Combine baking mix, milk, egg and vanilla in medium bowl; mix well. Gently fold in blueberries. (Batter will be stiff.) Spread batter in prepared pan; sprinkle with sausage pieces.

3. Bake 22 minutes or until top is lightly browned. Serve with maple syrup.

Makes 6 servings

OVEN PORK CASSOULET

- 1 tablespoon canola oil
- 1¼ pounds pork tenderloin, trimmed and cut into 1-inch pieces
- 1 cup chopped onion
- 1 cup chopped carrots
- 3 cloves garlic, minced
- 2 cans (about 15 ounces each) cannellini beans, rinsed and drained
- 1 can (about 14 ounces) diced tomatoes with Italian seasoning
- 4 ounces smoked sausage, cut into ¼-inch-thick slices
- 1 teaspoon dried thyme
- ½ teaspoon salt
- ¼ teaspoon dried rosemary
- ¼ teaspoon black pepper

1. Preheat oven to 325°F.

2. Heat oil in large skillet over medium heat; brown pork in batches. Transfer to plate.

3. Add onion, carrots and garlic to skillet; cook and stir 8 to 10 minutes or until tender. Combine pork, onion mixture, beans, tomatoes, sausage, thyme, salt, rosemary and pepper in 3-quart casserole; mix well.

4. Cover and bake 35 to 40 minutes or until pork is barely pink in center.

Makes 8 servings

Sausage, Beef & Bean Casserole

Prep Time: 15 minutes ☰ Bake Time: 30 minutes ☰ Total Time: 45 minutes

- 1 **pound sweet *or* hot Italian pork sausage, cut into 1-inch pieces**
- ½ **pound ground beef**
- 1 **small onion, chopped (about ¼ cup)**
- 1 **bag (6 ounces) fresh baby spinach**
- 1 **can (10½ ounces) CAMPBELL'S® Condensed Cream of Mushroom Soup (Regular *or* 98% Fat Free)**
- ¼ **cup milk**
- 1 **can (about 15 ounces) cannellini beans, rinsed and drained**
- 1 **cup PEPPERIDGE FARM® Herb Seasoned Stuffing**
- ½ **cup crumbled blue cheese *or* shredded Cheddar cheese (about 2 ounces)**

1. Heat the oven to 350°F.

2. Cook the sausage, beef and onion in a 12-inch nonstick skillet or 5-quart saucepan until the sausage and beef are well browned, stirring often to break up beef. Pour off any fat. Stir in the spinach and cook until the spinach is wilted.

3. Stir the soup, milk and beans into the skillet. Spoon the mixture into a 2-quart casserole.

4. Stir the stuffing and cheese in a small bowl. Sprinkle around the edge of the dish.

5. Bake for 30 minutes or until the sausage mixture is hot and bubbling.

Makes 6 servings

KITCHEN TIP: If your skillet has a handle that is not oven-safe, cover it with aluminum foil to protect it in the oven.

Tuscan Baked Rigatoni

- 1 pound bulk Italian sausage
- 1 package (16 ounces) uncooked rigatoni pasta, cooked, drained and kept warm
- 2 cups (8 ounces) shredded fontina cheese
- 2 tablespoons olive oil
- 2 bulbs fennel, thinly sliced
- 4 cloves garlic, minced
- 1 can (28 ounces) crushed tomatoes
- 1 cup whipping cream
- 1 teaspoon salt
- 1 teaspoon black pepper
- 8 cups packed fresh spinach
- 1 can (about 15 ounces) cannellini beans, rinsed and drained
- 2 tablespoons pine nuts
- ½ cup grated Parmesan cheese

1. Preheat oven to 350°F. Spray 4-quart casserole with nonstick cooking spray.

2. Brown sausage in large skillet over medium-high heat, stirring to break up meat. Drain fat. Transfer to prepared casserole. Add pasta and fontina; mix well.

3. Heat oil in same skillet. Add fennel and garlic; cook and stir over medium heat 3 minutes or until fennel is tender. Add tomatoes, cream, salt and pepper; cook and stir until slightly thickened. Stir in spinach, beans and pine nuts; cook until heated through. Pour over pasta mixture; toss to coat. Sprinkle with Parmesan.

4. Bake 30 minutes or until bubbly and heated through.

Makes 6 to 8 servings

Sausage and Polenta Casserole

- 1 tablespoon olive oil
- 1 onion, diced
- 1 red bell pepper, diced
- 1 cup chopped mushrooms
- 1 pound bulk Italian sausage
- 1 jar (28 to 30 ounces) meatless pasta sauce
- 1 roll (16 to 18 ounces) polenta, cut crosswise into 9 slices
- ¼ cup grated Parmesan cheese

1. Preheat oven to 350°F. Spray 8-inch square baking dish with nonstick cooking spray.

2. Heat oil in large skillet over medium heat. Add onion, bell pepper and mushrooms; cook and stir 5 minutes or until tender. Add sausage; cook and stir until browned, breaking up sausage into small pieces with spoon. Drain fat. Stir in pasta sauce; cook 5 minutes.

3. Place polenta slices in prepared baking dish; top with sausage mixture.

4. Bake 15 minutes or until heated through. Sprinkle with cheese.

Makes 4 servings

SAVORY VEGETABLE STUFFING BAKE

PREP TIME: 20 minutes ☰ BAKE TIME: 30 minutes ☰ TOTAL TIME: 50 minutes

- ¼ pound bulk pork sausage
- 1 large onion, chopped (about 1 cup)
- ½ teaspoon dried thyme leaves, crushed
- 1 can (10¾ ounces) CAMPBELL'S® Condensed Cream of Celery Soup (Regular *or* 98% Fat Free)
- 1 can (about 8 ounces) stewed tomatoes
- 2 cups frozen vegetable combination (broccoli, corn, red pepper)
- 3 cups PEPPERIDGE FARM® Herb Seasoned Stuffing

1. Heat the oven to 350°F. Cook the sausage, onion and thyme in a 12-inch skillet over medium-high heat until the sausage is browned, stirring frequently to separate the meat. Pour off any fat.

2. Stir the soup, tomatoes and vegetables into the skillet. Heat to a boil. Remove the skillet from the heat. Add the stuffing and stir lightly to coat. Spoon into a 1½-quart casserole.

3. Bake for 30 minutes or until hot and bubbling.

Makes 6 servings

Hash Brown Casserole

- 1 package (32 ounces) refrigerated diced potatoes, thawed
- 1 container (16 ounces) sour cream
- 1 can (10½ ounces) condensed cream of chicken soup, undiluted
- 1½ cups (6 ounces) shredded sharp Cheddar cheese
- ¾ cup thinly sliced green onions
- 4 slices bacon, crisp-cooked and crumbled
- 2 teaspoons hot pepper sauce
- ¼ teaspoon garlic salt

1. Preheat oven to 350°F. Spray 13×9-inch baking dish with nonstick cooking spray.

2. Combine potatoes, sour cream, soup, cheese, green onions, bacon, hot pepper sauce and garlic salt in large bowl; mix well. Transfer to prepared baking dish.

3. Bake 55 to 60 minutes or until potatoes are tender and cooked through. Stir before serving.

Makes about 10 servings

6 Cheese Italian Sausage & Pasta

Prep Time: 20 minutes ☰ Cook Time: 25 minutes

- 1 pound mild or hot Italian sausage
- 1 large onion, coarsely chopped
- 2 cloves garlic, minced
- 1 each: large red and green bell peppers, cut into 1-inch squares
- 1 can (14½ ounces) diced tomatoes or Italian-style tomatoes, undrained
- 1 can (6 ounces) tomato paste
- 8 ounces ziti or mostaccioli pasta, cooked and drained
- ¼ cup chopped fresh basil or 2 teaspoons dried basil
- 2 cups (8 ounces) SARGENTO® Chef Blends™ Shredded 6 Cheese Italian, divided

CUT sausage into ½-inch pieces; discard casings. Cook sausage in large skillet over medium heat 5 minutes or until browned on all sides. Pour off drippings. Add onion, garlic and bell peppers; cook 5 minutes or until sausage is cooked through and vegetables are crisp-tender.

ADD tomatoes and tomato paste; mix well. Stir in pasta, basil and 1 cup cheese. Transfer to 13×9-inch baking dish. Cover and bake in preheated 375°F oven 20 minutes. Uncover; sprinkle remaining cheese evenly over casserole. Continue to bake 5 minutes or until cheese is melted.

Makes 6 servings

Ham and Cheese Puff Pie

2 cups (about 1 pound) diced cooked ham

1 package (10 ounces) frozen chopped spinach, thawed and squeezed dry

½ cup diced red bell pepper

4 green onions, sliced

3 eggs

¾ cup all-purpose flour

¾ cup (3 ounces) shredded Swiss cheese

¾ cup milk

1 tablespoon prepared mustard

1 teaspoon grated lemon peel

1 teaspoon dried dill weed

½ teaspoon garlic salt

½ teaspoon black pepper

1. Preheat oven to 425°F. Spray 2-quart round casserole with nonstick cooking spray.

2. Combine ham, spinach, bell pepper and green onions in prepared casserole. Beat eggs in medium bowl. Stir in flour, cheese, milk, mustard, lemon peel, dill weed, garlic salt and black pepper until blended; pour over ham mixture.

3. Bake 30 to 35 minutes or until puffed and browned.

Makes 4 to 6 servings

POULTRY

CLASSIC TURKEY POT PIE

2 cans (15 ounces each) VEG•ALL® Original Mixed Vegetables, drained

1 can (10¾ ounces) condensed cream of potato soup, undiluted

¼ cup milk

1 pound cooked turkey, shredded (2 cups)

¼ teaspoon dried thyme

¼ teaspoon black pepper

2 (9-inch) refrigerated ready-to-bake pie crusts

Preheat oven to 375°F. In medium mixing bowl, combine first 6 ingredients; mix well. Place 1 pie crust into 9-inch pie pan; pour vegetable mixture into pie crust. Top with remaining crust, crimp edges to seal and slit top with knife. Bake for 50 to 60 minutes (on lower rack) or until crust is golden brown and filling is hot. Allow pie to cool slightly before cutting into wedges to serve.

Makes 8 servings

Greek Chicken, Spinach and Rice Bake

2 tablespoons olive oil, divided

1 cup finely chopped onion

1 package (10 ounces) frozen chopped spinach, thawed and squeezed dry

1 cup uncooked quick-cooking brown rice

1 cup water

½ teaspoon salt

⅛ teaspoon ground red pepper

12 ounces chicken tenders

2 teaspoons Greek seasoning (oregano, rosemary and sage mixture)

½ teaspoon lemon-pepper seasoning

1 lemon, cut into wedges

1. Preheat oven to 350°F.

2. Heat 1 tablespoon oil in large ovenproof skillet over medium heat. Add onion; cook and stir 2 minutes or until translucent. Add spinach, rice, water, salt and red pepper; stir until well blended. Remove from heat.

3. Place chicken on top of rice mixture in single layer; sprinkle with Greek seasoning and lemon-pepper seasoning.

4. Cover with foil and bake 25 minutes or until chicken is no longer pink in center. Drizzle with remaining 1 tablespoon oil; serve with lemon wedges.

Makes 4 servings

Cacciatore Noodle Casserole

PREP TIME: 10 minutes ☰ BAKE TIME: 25 minutes

2 cups PREGO® Traditional Italian Sauce

¾ cup water

1 cup frozen Italian-style vegetable combination

1 jar (4½ ounces) sliced mushrooms, drained

3 cups cubed cooked chicken

3 cups medium egg noodles, cooked and drained

¼ cup grated Parmesan cheese

1. Heat the oven to 400°F. Stir the Italian sauce, water, Italian vegetables, mushrooms, chicken and noodles in a 2-quart casserole.

2. Bake for 25 minutes or until hot. Stir.

3. Sprinkle with Parmesan cheese. Serve immediately.

Makes 6 servings

EASY SUBSTITUTION TIP: Substitute leftover cubed rotisserie chicken or **2 cans (12.5 ounces each)** SWANSON® Premium White Chunk Chicken Breast, drained.

CHIPOTLE TURKEY STRATA

    6 to 8 slices Italian bread (½ inch thick)

    2 tablespoons chipotle sauce*

    2 cups chopped cooked dark turkey meat

 1½ cups (6 ounces) shredded Cheddar cheese, divided

    5 eggs

 2½ cups milk

    ½ teaspoon salt

    ¼ teaspoon black pepper

If you can't find chipotle sauce, substitute 1 tablespoon tomato sauce mixed with 1 tablespoon adobo sauce from canned chipotle chiles.

1. Preheat oven to 325°F. Spray 9-inch square baking pan with nonstick cooking spray.

2. Arrange 3 to 4 bread slices to cover bottom of pan, cutting bread to fit, if necessary. Spread chipotle sauce over bread; top with turkey, 1 cup cheese and remaining 3 to 4 bread slices.

3. Beat eggs, milk, salt and pepper in medium bowl until blended. Pour over bread; press down firmly so bread absorbs liquid. Top with remaining ½ cup cheese.

4. Bake 60 to 70 minutes or until set and golden brown. Let stand 10 to 15 minutes before cutting.

Makes 6 servings

TIP: This dish can be assembled up to 8 hours in advance. Cover with foil and refrigerate until ready to bake.

COUNTRY CHICKEN AND BISCUITS

1 can (10.75 ounces) condensed cream of celery soup

⅓ cup milk or water

4 boneless, skinless chicken breast halves, cooked and cut into bite-sized pieces

1 can (14.5 ounces) DEL MONTE® Cut Green Beans, drained

Black pepper (optional)

1 can (11 ounces) refrigerated biscuits

1. Preheat oven to 375°F.

2. Combine soup and milk in large bowl. Gently stir in chicken and green beans; season with pepper, if desired. Spoon into 11×7-inch or 2-quart baking dish.

3. Cover with foil and bake at 375°F 20 to 25 minutes or until hot.

4. Separate biscuit dough into individual biscuits. Immediately arrange biscuits over hot chicken mixture. Bake about 15 minutes or until biscuits are golden brown and baked through.

Makes 4 servings

MICROWAVE DIRECTIONS: To prepare this dish even faster, use a microwavable baking dish in step 2. Cover with plastic wrap; slit to vent. Microwave on HIGH 8 to 10 minutes or until heated through, rotating dish once. Continue as directed in step 4.

TURKEY APPLE CRANBERRY BAKE

PREP TIME: 20 minutes ☰ BAKE TIME: 30 minutes ☰ TOTAL TIME: 50 minutes

1 cup PEPPERIDGE FARM® Herb Seasoned Stuffing

1 tablespoon butter, melted

1 can (10¾ ounces) CAMPBELL'S® Condensed Cream of Celery Soup (Regular *or* 98% Fat Free)

½ cup milk

2 cups cubed cooked turkey

1 medium apple, diced (about 1½ cups)

1 stalk celery, finely chopped (about ½ cup)

½ cup dried cranberries

½ cup pecan halves, chopped

1. Heat the oven to 400°F. Stir the stuffing and butter in a small bowl. Set aside.

2. Stir the soup, milk, turkey, apple, celery, cranberries and pecans in a 12×8×2-inch shallow baking dish. Sprinkle the reserved stuffing mixture over the turkey mixture.

3. Bake for 30 minutes or until hot and bubbling.

Makes 4 servings

Artichoke-Olive Chicken Casserole

1 tablespoon olive oil

1 medium onion, chopped

½ green bell pepper, chopped

1½ cups uncooked rotini pasta, cooked and drained

2 cups shredded cooked chicken

1 can (about 14 ounces) diced tomatoes with Italian seasoning

1 can (14 ounces) artichoke hearts, drained and quartered

1 can (6 ounces) sliced black olives, drained

1 teaspoon Italian seasoning

2 cups (8 ounces) shredded mozzarella cheese

1. Preheat oven to 350°F. Spray 2-quart casserole with nonstick cooking spray.

2. Heat oil in large skillet over medium heat. Add onion and bell pepper; cook and stir 1 minute. Add pasta, chicken, tomatoes, artichokes, olives and Italian seasoning; stir gently until blended.

3. Place half of chicken mixture in prepared casserole; sprinkle with half of cheese. Top with remaining chicken mixture and cheese.

4. Cover and bake 35 minutes or until hot and bubbly.

Makes 8 servings

Spicy Turkey Bake

- 1 tablespoon olive oil
- 1 pound turkey breast cutlets, cut into ½-inch pieces
- 2 spicy turkey or chicken sausages (about 3 ounces each), cut into ½-inch-thick slices
- 1 cup diced green bell pepper
- ½ cup sliced mushrooms
- ½ cup diced onion
- 1 jalapeño pepper,* minced (optional)
- ½ cup chicken broth or water
- 1 can (about 14 ounces) diced tomatoes
- 1 cup cooked egg noodles
- 1 teaspoon Italian seasoning
- ½ teaspoon paprika
- ¼ teaspoon black pepper
- 6 tablespoons grated Parmesan cheese
- 2 tablespoons plain dry bread crumbs

Jalapeño peppers can sting and irritate the skin, so wear rubber gloves when handling peppers and do not touch your eyes.

1. Preheat oven to 350°F.

2. Heat oil in large nonstick skillet over medium heat. Add turkey and sausages; cook and stir 2 minutes. Add bell pepper, mushrooms, onion and jalapeño, if desired; cook and stir 5 minutes.

3. Add broth; cook 1 minute, stirring to scrape up browned bits from bottom of skillet. Add tomatoes, noodles, Italian seasoning, paprika and black pepper; mix well. Transfer to shallow 10-inch oval or round casserole; sprinkle with cheese and bread crumbs.

4. Bake 15 to 20 minutes or until heated through and bread crumbs are golden brown.

Makes 6 servings

Chicken & Roasted Garlic Risotto

Prep Time: 5 minutes ☰ Bake Time: 40 minutes ☰ Stand Time: 5 minutes

- 1 can (10½ ounces) CAMPBELL'S® Condensed Cream of Chicken Soup (Regular *or* 98% Fat Free)
- 1 can (10½ ounces) CAMPBELL'S Condensed Cream of Mushroom with Roasted Garlic Soup
- 2 cups water
- 1 package (10 ounces) frozen peas and carrots (about 2 cups)
- 1 cup *uncooked* regular long-grain white rice
- 6 skinless, boneless chicken breast halves (about 1½ pounds)
- ¼ cup grated Parmesan cheese

1. Heat the oven to 375°F.

2. Stir the soups, water, vegetables and rice in a 13×9×2-inch (3-quart) shallow baking dish. Top with the chicken. Cover.

3. Bake for 40 minutes or until the chicken is cooked through. Sprinkle with the cheese. Let stand for 5 minutes.

Makes 6 servings

KITCHEN TIP: Traditionally, risotto is made by sautéing rice in butter, then stirring broth into the rice a little at a time—very labor-intensive. This dish gives you the same creamy texture with a lot less work!

CHILI WAGON WHEEL CASSEROLE

2 teaspoons vegetable oil

1 pound ground turkey or ground beef

¾ cup chopped onion

¾ cup chopped green bell pepper

1 can (about 14 ounces) stewed tomatoes

1 can (8 ounces) tomato sauce

½ teaspoon black pepper

¼ teaspoon ground allspice

8 ounces uncooked wagon wheel or other pasta, cooked and drained

½ cup (2 ounces) shredded Cheddar cheese

1. Preheat oven to 350°F.

2. Heat oil in large nonstick skillet over medium-high heat. Add turkey; cook and stir 5 minutes or until no longer pink. Add onion and bell pepper; cook and stir until tender. (Drain fat if using ground beef.)

3. Stir in tomatoes, tomato sauce, black pepper and allspice; cook 2 minutes. Stir in pasta until coated. Transfer to 2½-quart casserole; sprinkle with cheese.

4. Bake 20 to 25 minutes or until heated through.

Makes 6 servings

CREAMY CHICKEN FLORENTINE

PREP TIME: 15 minutes ☰ BAKE TIME: 40 minutes ☰ STAND TIME: 5 minutes

1 can (10½ ounces) CAMPBELL'S® Condensed Cream of Chicken Soup (Regular *or* 98% Fat Free)

1½ cups water

½ of a 20-ounce bag frozen cut leaf spinach, thawed and well drained (about 3½ cups)

1 can (about 14½ ounces) Italian-style diced tomatoes

4 skinless, boneless chicken breast halves (about 1 pound), cut into 1-inch cubes

2½ cups *uncooked* penne pasta

½ cup shredded mozzarella cheese (about 2 ounces)

1. Heat the oven to 375°F. Stir the soup, water, spinach, tomatoes and chicken in a 3-quart shallow baking dish. Cover.

2. Bake for 20 minutes. Cook the pasta according to the package directions and drain well in a colander. Uncover the baking dish and stir in the pasta.

3. Bake for 20 minutes or until the pasta mixture is hot and bubbling. Sprinkle with the cheese. Let stand for 5 minutes or until the cheese is melted.

Makes 4 servings

Chicken Zucchini Casserole

- 1 package (about 6 ounces) herb-flavored stuffing mix
- ½ cup (1 stick) butter, melted
- 2 cups cubed zucchini
- 1½ cups chopped cooked chicken
- 1 can (10¾ ounces) condensed cream of celery soup, undiluted
- 1 cup grated carrots
- 1 onion, chopped
- ½ cup sour cream
- ½ cup (2 ounces) shredded Cheddar cheese

1. Preheat oven to 350°F.

2. Combine stuffing mix and butter in 13×9-inch baking dish. Remove 1 cup stuffing; set aside.

3. Combine zucchini, chicken, soup, carrots, onion and sour cream in large bowl; mix well. Pour over stuffing in baking dish; top with reserved 1 cup stuffing and cheese.

4. Bake 40 to 45 minutes or until heated through and cheese is melted.

Makes 8 servings

SEAFOOD

SEAFOOD PASTA BAKE

½ **cup olive oil**

1 **pound asparagus, trimmed and cut into 1-inch pieces**

1 **cup chopped green onions**

1 **tablespoon plus 2 teaspoons minced garlic**

1 **package (16 ounces) linguine, cooked and drained**

1 **pound medium cooked shrimp, peeled**

1 **package (8 ounces) imitation crabmeat**

1 **package (8 ounces) imitation lobster**

1 **can (8 ounces) pitted black olives, drained**

1. Preheat oven to 350°F. Spray 4-quart casserole with nonstick cooking spray.

2. Heat oil in large skillet over medium heat. Add asparagus, green onions and garlic; cook and stir until vegetables are tender.

3. Combine asparagus mixture, linguine, shrimp, crabmeat, lobster and olives in prepared casserole.

4. Bake 30 minutes or until heated through.

Makes 6 servings

Classic Tuna Noodle Casserole

PREP TIME: 20 minutes ☰ BAKE TIME: 25 minutes ☰ TOTAL TIME: 35 minutes

1 can (10½ ounces) CAMPBELL'S® Condensed Cream of Celery Soup (Regular *or* 98% Fat Free)

½ cup milk

1 cup frozen peas

2 tablespoons chopped pimientos

2 cans (about 5 ounces *each*) tuna in water, drained and flaked

4 ounces (about 2 cups) medium egg noodles, cooked and drained

2 tablespoons dry bread crumbs

1 tablespoon butter, melted

1. Heat the oven to 400°F. Stir the soup, milk, peas, pimientos, tuna and noodles in a 1½-quart baking dish. Stir the bread crumbs and butter in a small bowl.

2. Bake for 20 minutes or until the tuna mixture is hot and bubbling. Stir the tuna mixture. Sprinkle with the bread crumb mixture.

3. Bake for 5 minutes or until the bread crumbs are golden brown.

Makes 4 servings

SERVING SUGGESTION: Serve with your favorite vegetable combination. For dessert serve ice cream.

KITCHEN TIP: Substitute CAMPBELL'S® Condensed Cream of Mushroom Soup for the Cream of Celery Soup.

Lemon Shrimp

1 package (12 ounces) uncooked egg noodles, cooked and drained

½ cup (1 stick) butter, softened

2 pounds medium cooked shrimp, peeled

3 tomatoes, chopped

1 cup chicken broth

1 cup shredded carrots

1 can (4 ounces) sliced mushrooms, drained

2 tablespoons lemon juice

2 cloves garlic, minced

½ teaspoon celery seed

¼ teaspoon black pepper

1. Preheat oven to 350°F.

2. Combine noodles and butter in large bowl until butter is melted and noodles are evenly coated. Stir in shrimp, tomatoes, broth, carrots, mushrooms, lemon juice, garlic, celery seed and black pepper; mix well. Transfer to 3-quart casserole.

3. Bake 15 to 20 minutes or until heated through.

Makes 8 servings

CRUSTLESS SALMON AND BROCCOLI QUICHE

3 eggs

¼ cup chopped green onions

¼ cup plain yogurt

2 teaspoons all-purpose flour

1 teaspoon dried basil

⅛ teaspoon salt

⅛ teaspoon black pepper

¾ cup frozen broccoli florets, thawed and drained

1 can (6 ounces) boneless skinless salmon, drained and flaked

2 tablespoons grated Parmesan cheese

1 plum tomato, thinly sliced

¼ cup fresh bread crumbs

1. Preheat oven to 375°F. Spray 1½-quart casserole or 9-inch deep-dish pie plate with nonstick cooking spray.

2. Beat eggs, green onions, yogurt, flour, basil, salt and pepper in medium bowl until well blended. Stir in broccoli, salmon and cheese; mix well. Spread in prepared casserole; top with tomato slices and bread crumbs.

3. Bake 20 to 25 minutes or until knife inserted near center comes out clean. Let stand 5 minutes before serving.

Makes 4 servings

SEAFOOD NEWBURG CASSEROLE

- 1 can (10¾ ounces) condensed cream of shrimp soup, undiluted
- ½ cup half-and-half
- 1 tablespoon dry sherry
- ¼ teaspoon ground red pepper
- 2 cans (6 ounces each) lump crabmeat, drained
- 3 cups cooked rice
- 4 ounces medium raw shrimp, peeled
- 4 ounces bay scallops, rinsed and patted dry
- 1 jar (4 ounces) pimientos, drained and chopped
- ¼ cup finely chopped fresh parsley

1. Preheat oven to 350°F. Spray 2½-quart casserole with nonstick cooking spray.

2. Combine soup, half-and-half, sherry and red pepper in large bowl; mix well. Stir in crabmeat, rice, shrimp, scallops and pimientos until well blended. Transfer to prepared casserole.

3. Cover and bake 25 minutes or until shrimp and scallops are opaque. Sprinkle with parsley.

Makes 6 servings

Ham Jambalaya

2 tablespoons butter

1 onion, chopped

½ cup thinly sliced celery

½ red bell pepper, diced

2 cloves garlic, minced

1 jar (about 16 ounces) medium-hot salsa

2 cups cubed cooked ham

1 cup uncooked long grain rice

1 cup water

⅔ cup vegetable broth

3 teaspoons prepared horseradish

2 teaspoons honey

¼ to ½ teaspoon hot pepper sauce

1½ pounds large raw shrimp, peeled and deveined

1 tablespoon chopped fresh mint

1. Preheat oven to 350°F.

2. Melt butter in Dutch oven over medium heat. Add onion, celery, bell pepper and garlic; cook and stir 2 minutes or until vegetables are tender. Stir in salsa, ham, rice, water, broth, horseradish, honey and hot pepper sauce; mix well.

3. Cover and bake 40 minutes or until rice is almost tender.

4. Stir in shrimp and mint; bake 10 to 15 minutes or until shrimp are pink and opaque.

Makes 6 to 8 servings

SALMON NOODLE CASSEROLE

6 ounces uncooked wide egg noodles, cooked and drained

2 teaspoons vegetable oil

1 onion, finely chopped

¾ cup thinly sliced carrot

¾ cup thinly sliced celery

1 can (about 15 ounces) salmon, drained, skin and bones discarded

1 can (10¾ ounces) condensed cream of celery soup, undiluted

1 cup (4 ounces) shredded Cheddar cheese

¾ cup frozen peas

½ cup sour cream

¼ cup milk

2 teaspoons dried dill weed

Black pepper

1. Preheat oven to 350°F. Place noodles in 2-quart baking dish.

2. Heat oil in medium skillet over medium heat. Add onion, carrot and celery; cook and stir 5 minutes or until carrot is crisp-tender. Add to noodles with salmon, soup, cheese, peas, sour cream, milk and dill weed. Season with pepper; stir gently until blended.

3. Cover and bake 25 minutes or until hot and bubbly.

Makes 4 servings

SHRIMP CREOLE

2 tablespoons olive oil

1½ cups chopped green bell peppers

1 medium onion, chopped

⅔ cup chopped celery

2 cloves garlic, minced

1 cup uncooked rice

1 can (about 14 ounces) diced tomatoes, drained and liquid reserved

2 teaspoons hot pepper sauce or to taste

1 teaspoon dried oregano

¾ teaspoon salt

½ teaspoon dried thyme

Black pepper

1 pound medium raw shrimp, peeled

1 tablespoon chopped fresh parsley (optional)

1. Preheat oven to 325°F.

2. Heat oil in large skillet over medium-high heat. Add bell peppers, onion, celery and garlic; cook and stir 5 minutes or until vegetables are tender.

3. Add rice; cook and stir 5 minutes over medium heat. Stir in tomatoes, hot pepper sauce, oregano, salt and thyme. Season with black pepper; mix well. Pour reserved tomato liquid into measuring cup; add enough water to measure 1¾ cups. Add to skillet; cook and stir 2 minutes. Stir in shrimp. Transfer to 2½-quart Dutch oven or casserole.

4. Cover and bake 55 minutes or until rice is tender and liquid is absorbed. Garnish with parsley.

Makes 4 to 6 servings

Tuna Tomato Casserole

1 package (12 ounces) wide egg noodles, cooked and drained

2 cans (6 ounces each) tuna, drained and flaked

1 cup mayonnaise

1 onion, finely chopped

¼ teaspoon salt

¼ teaspoon black pepper

8 to 10 plum tomatoes, sliced ¼ inch thick

1 cup (4 ounces) shredded Cheddar or mozzarella cheese

1. Preheat oven to 375°F.

2. Combine noodles, tuna, mayonnaise, onion, salt and pepper in large bowl; mix well.

3. Layer half of noodle mixture, half of tomatoes and half of cheese in 13×9-inch baking dish; press down slightly. Repeat layers.

4. Bake 20 minutes or until cheese is melted and casserole is heated through.

Makes 6 servings

Cheesy Enchilada Shrimp

PREP TIME: 5 minutes ☰ START TO FINISH TIME: 20 minutes

1 can (10 ounces) ORTEGA® Enchilada Sauce, Mild
1 pound large shrimp, peeled
2 cups (8 ounces) shredded mozzarella cheese

PREHEAT oven to 400°F.

POUR half of enchilada sauce in bottom of 8- to 10-inch ovenproof serving dish. Top with peeled shrimp in single layer. Pour remaining enchilada sauce over shrimp. Sprinkle with cheese to cover.

BAKE 12 minutes or until cheese is melted and sauce begins to bubble. Serve warm with toothpicks.

Makes about 35 shrimp

TIP: Use these shrimp for a filling for ORTEGA® Fiesta Flats.

VEGETABLES

SPINACH-CHEESE PASTA CASSEROLE

2 eggs

1 cup ricotta cheese

1 package (10 ounces) frozen chopped spinach, thawed and squeezed dry

1 jar (26 ounces) marinara sauce

8 ounces uncooked shell pasta, cooked and drained

1 teaspoon salt

1 cup (4 ounces) shredded mozzarella cheese

¼ cup grated Parmesan cheese

1. Preheat oven to 350°F. Spray 1½-quart casserole with nonstick cooking spray.

2. Beat eggs in large bowl. Add ricotta and spinach; beat until well blended. Add marinara sauce, pasta and salt; stir gently until pasta is well coated. Transfer to prepared casserole; sprinkle with mozzarella and Parmesan.

3. Cover and bake 30 minutes. Uncover; bake 15 minutes or until hot and bubbly.

Makes 6 to 8 servings

HUEVOS RANCHEROS CASSEROLE

  6 corn tortillas

  1 cup refried black beans

  1 cup salsa

  10 eggs

  ¾ cup milk

  1 cup (4 ounces) shredded Mexican cheese blend

1. Preheat oven to 400°F. Spray 13×9-inch baking dish with nonstick cooking spray.

2. Line prepared baking dish with tortillas, overlapping as necessary. Spread beans over tortillas; spread salsa over beans.

3. Beat eggs and milk in large bowl until blended. Pour over beans and salsa; sprinkle with cheese.

4. Cover with foil and bake 30 minutes. Uncover; bake 5 minutes or until center is set and edges are lightly browned and pulling away from sides of dish.

Makes 6 to 8 servings

SERVING SUGGESTION: Serve with additional salsa, sour cream, chopped fresh cilantro and sliced avocado.

NEAPOLITAN PASTA SHELLS

PREP TIME: 20 minutes ☰ BAKE TIME: 30 minutes ☰ TOTAL TIME: 50 minutes

- 2 tablespoons vegetable oil
- 2 medium zucchini, sliced (about 3 cups)
- 2 cups sliced mushrooms
- 1 medium onion, chopped (about ½ cup)
- ¼ teaspoon ground black pepper
- 2 cups PREGO® Three Cheese Italian Sauce
- ½ of a 16-ounce package medium shell-shaped pasta, cooked and drained (4 cups)
- 1 cup shredded mozzarella cheese

1. Heat the oven to 350°F. Heat the oil in a 3-quart saucepan over medium heat. Add the zucchini, mushrooms, onion and pepper and cook until the vegetables are tender-crisp.

2. Stir the Italian sauce and pasta into the saucepan. Spoon into a 2-quart baking dish. Sprinkle with the cheese.

3. Bake for 30 minutes or until hot and bubbling.

Makes 4 servings

Red, White and Black Bean Casserole

2 tablespoons olive oil

1 yellow or green bell pepper, cut into ½-inch strips

½ cup sliced green onions

1 can (14½ ounces) chunky-style salsa

1 can (4 ounces) diced green chiles, drained

1 package (1½ ounces) taco seasoning mix

2 tablespoons chopped fresh cilantro

½ teaspoon salt

2 cups cooked rice

1 can (19 ounces) white cannellini beans, rinsed and drained

1 can (about 15 ounces) red kidney beans, rinsed and drained

1 can (about 15 ounces) black beans, rinsed and drained

1 cup (4 ounces) shredded Cheddar cheese, divided

1 package (6-inch) flour tortillas

1. Preheat oven to 350°F. Spray 1½-quart casserole with nonstick cooking spray.

2. Heat oil in large saucepan over medium-high heat. Add bell pepper and green onions; cook and stir about 5 minutes. Add salsa, chiles, taco seasoning mix, cilantro and salt; cook 5 minutes, stirring occasionally. Stir in rice and beans. Remove from heat; stir in ½ cup cheese. Transfer to prepared casserole; sprinkle with remaining ½ cup cheese.

3. Cover and bake 30 to 40 minutes or until heated through. Serve with warm tortillas.

Makes 6 servings

EGG AND GREEN CHILE RICE BAKE

¾ cup uncooked instant brown rice, cooked according to package directions

½ cup chopped green onions

1 can (4 ounces) diced green chiles, drained

½ teaspoon ground cumin

¼ teaspoon salt

4 eggs, beaten

½ cup (2 ounces) shredded sharp Cheddar cheese or Mexican cheese blend

½ cup pico de gallo

1 lime, cut into wedges

1. Preheat oven to 350°F. Spray 8-inch square baking dish with nonstick cooking spray.

2. Combine rice, green onions, chiles, cumin and salt in prepared baking dish; mix well. Pour eggs evenly over top.

3. Bake 30 to 35 minutes or until center is set. Sprinkle with cheese; bake 3 minutes or until cheese is melted. Let stand 5 minutes before serving. Serve with pico de gallo and lime wedges.

Makes 4 servings

BAKED PASTA PRIMAVERA CASSEROLE

PREP TIME: 20 minutes ☰ COOK TIME: 30 minutes

1 jar (1 pound 8 ounces) RAGÚ® OLD WORLD STYLE® Pasta Sauce

2 cups shredded mozzarella cheese (about 8 ounces), divided

½ cup grated Parmesan cheese

1 bag (16 ounces) frozen Italian-style vegetables, thawed

8 ounces ziti or penne pasta, cooked and drained

1. Preheat oven to 350°F.

2. Combine Pasta Sauce, 1 cup mozzarella cheese and Parmesan cheese in large bowl. Stir in vegetables and hot ziti.

3. Spoon pasta mixture into 2½-quart casserole; sprinkle with remaining 1 cup mozzarella cheese. Bake uncovered 30 minutes or until heated through.

Makes 6 servings

SPINACH AND MUSHROOM FRITTATA

PREP TIME: 10 minutes ☰ BAKE TIME: 35 minutes ☰ TOTAL TIME: 45 minutes

Vegetable cooking spray

10 eggs

1 can (10½ ounces) CAMPBELL'S® Condensed Cream of Mushroom Soup (Regular *or* 98% Fat Free)

1 package (10 ounces) frozen chopped spinach, thawed and well drained

1½ cups shredded Swiss cheese *or* Jarlsberg cheese (about 6 ounces)

½ teaspoon ground black pepper

1. Heat the oven to 375°F. Spray a 2-quart shallow baking dish with the cooking spray.

2. Beat the eggs in a large bowl with a fork or whisk. Stir in the soup. Stir in the spinach, **1 cup** cheese and black pepper. Pour the egg mixture into the baking dish.

3. Bake for 35 minutes or until set. Sprinkle with the remaining cheese.

Makes 8 servings

KITCHEN TIP: Make Ahead: Prepare the frittata as directed above, then cover and refrigerate for up to 24 hours. Before serving, remove the frittata from the refrigerator and let stand for about 30 minutes. Heat the oven to 350°F. Bake for 20 minutes or until hot.

CHILE CORN QUICHE

1 unbaked 9-inch pie crust

1 can (8¾ ounces) whole kernel corn, drained,
    or 1 cup frozen whole kernel corn, cooked

1 can (4 ounces) diced green chiles, drained

¼ cup thinly sliced green onions

1 cup (4 ounces) shredded Monterey Jack cheese

1½ cups half-and-half

3 eggs

½ teaspoon salt

½ teaspoon ground cumin

1. Preheat oven to 450°F. Line crust with foil; fill with dried beans or rice. Bake 10 minutes. Remove foil and beans; bake 5 minutes or until lightly browned. Cool on wire rack. *Reduce oven temperature to 375°F.*

2. Meanwhile, combine corn, chiles and green onions in medium bowl; mix well. Spoon into crust; sprinkle with cheese. Beat half-and-half, eggs, salt and cumin in same bowl until well blended. Pour over cheese.

3. Bake 35 to 45 minutes or until filling is puffed and knife inserted into center comes out clean. Let stand 10 minutes before serving.

Makes 6 servings

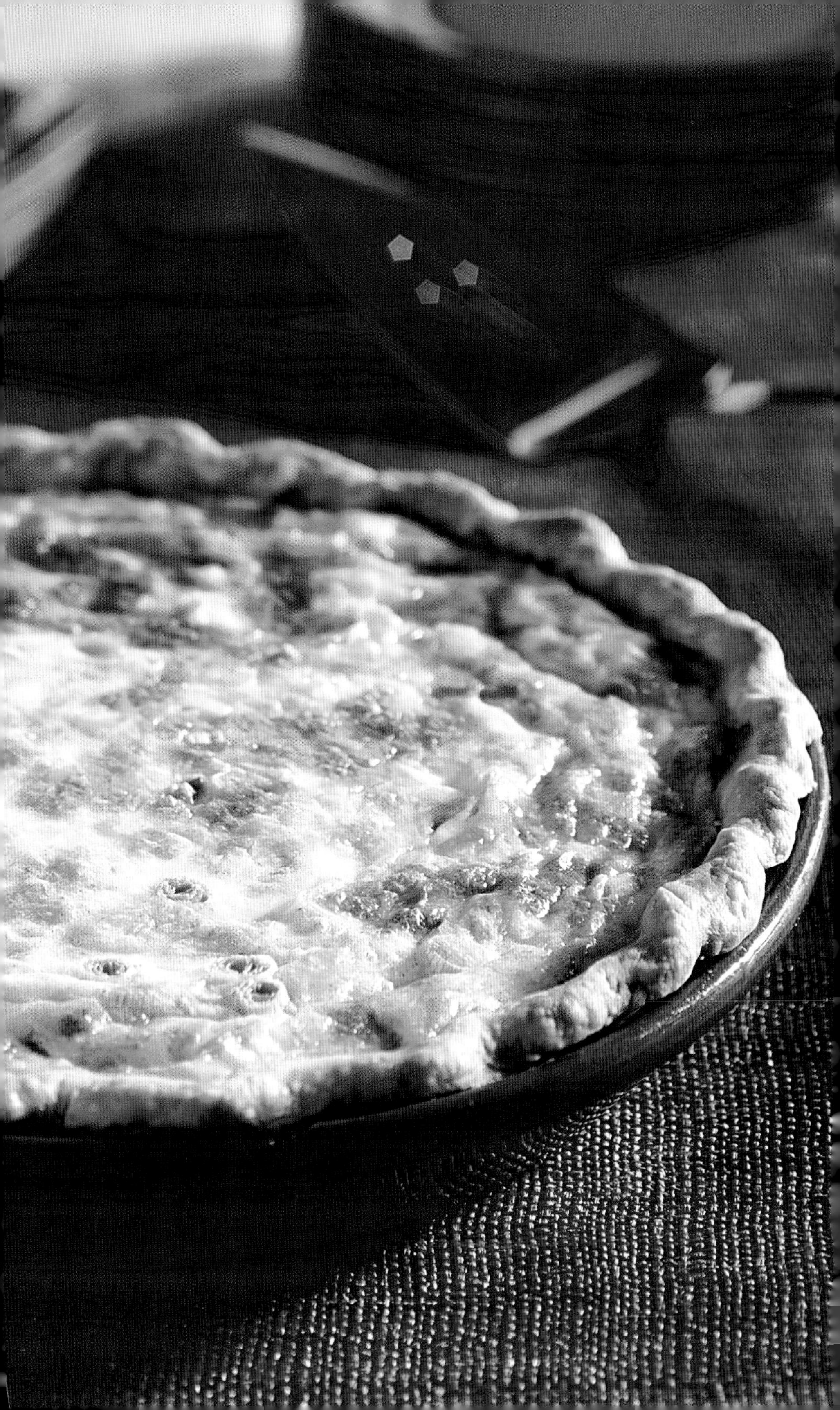

ZUCCHINI FETA CASSEROLE

1 tablespoon butter

4 medium zucchini, grated and drained in colander

2 eggs, beaten

½ cup grated Parmesan cheese

⅓ cup crumbled feta cheese

2 tablespoons chopped fresh parsley

1 tablespoon all-purpose flour

2 teaspoons chopped fresh marjoram

Dash hot pepper sauce

Salt and black pepper

1. Preheat oven to 375°F. Spray 2-quart casserole with nonstick cooking spray.

2. Melt butter in medium skillet over medium heat. Add zucchini; cook and stir until slightly browned. Remove from heat; stir in eggs, Parmesan, feta, parsley, flour, marjoram and hot pepper sauce. Season with salt and black pepper; mix well. Transfer to prepared casserole.

3. Bake 35 minutes or until hot and bubbly.

Makes 4 servings

Pasta and White Bean Bake

1 tablespoon olive oil

½ cup chopped onion

2 cloves garlic, minced

2 cans (about 15 ounces each) cannellini beans, rinsed and drained

3 cups cooked small shell pasta

1 can (8 ounces) tomato sauce

1½ teaspoons Italian seasoning

½ teaspoon salt

½ teaspoon black pepper

1 cup (4 ounces) shredded Italian cheese blend

2 tablespoons finely chopped fresh Italian parsley

1. Preheat oven to 350°F. Spray 2-quart casserole with nonstick cooking spray.

2. Heat oil in large skillet over medium-high heat. Add onion and garlic; cook and stir 4 minutes or until onion is tender.

3. Add beans, pasta, tomato sauce, Italian seasoning, salt and pepper; mix well. Transfer to prepared casserole; sprinkle with cheese and parsley.

4. Bake 20 minutes or until cheese is melted.

Makes 6 servings

Broccoli & Cheese Casserole

Prep Time: 15 minutes ☰ Bake Time: 30 minutes ☰ Stand Time: 5 minutes

1 can (10½ ounces) CAMPBELL'S® Condensed Cream of Mushroom Soup (Regular *or* 98% Fat Free)

½ cup milk

2 teaspoons yellow mustard

1 bag (16 ounces) frozen broccoli cuts, thawed and well drained

1 cup shredded Cheddar cheese (about 4 ounces)

⅓ cup dry bread crumbs

2 teaspoons butter, melted

1. Heat the oven to 350°F. Stir the soup, milk, mustard, broccoli and cheese in a 1½-quart casserole.

2. Stir the bread crumbs and butter in a small bowl. Sprinkle the crumb mixture over the broccoli mixture.

3. Bake for 30 minutes or until the broccoli is tender. Let stand for 5 minutes before serving.

Makes 6 servings

RICE IS NICE: Add **2 cups** cooked white rice to the broccoli mixture before baking.

CHEESE CHANGE-UP: Substitute mozzarella cheese for the Cheddar.

CHILE CHEESE PUFF

9 eggs

4 cups (16 ounces) shredded Monterey Jack cheese

2 cups (16 ounces) cottage cheese

2 cans (4 ounces each) diced green chiles, drained

1½ teaspoons sugar

¼ teaspoon salt

⅛ teaspoon hot pepper sauce

¾ cup all-purpose flour

1½ teaspoons baking powder

1 cup salsa

1. Preheat oven to 350°F. Spray 13×9-inch baking dish with nonstick cooking spray.

2. Beat eggs in large bowl. Add Monterey Jack, cottage cheese, chiles, sugar, salt and hot pepper sauce; beat until well blended. Add flour and baking powder; stir just until blended. Pour into prepared baking dish.

3. Bake 45 minutes or until set. Let stand 5 minutes before serving. Top with salsa.

Makes 8 servings

Saucy Vegetable Casserole

PREP TIME: 5 minutes ☰ COOK TIME: 20 minutes

2 bags (16 ounces each) frozen mixed vegetables (broccoli, cauliflower, carrots), thawed

2 cups FRENCH'S® French Fried Onions, divided

1 package (16 ounces) pasteurized process cheese, cut into ¼-inch slices

1. Preheat oven to 350°F. Combine vegetables and *1 cup* French Fried Onions in shallow 3-quart baking dish. Top evenly with cheese slices.

2. Bake 15 minutes or until hot and cheese is almost melted; stir. Top with remaining *1 cup* onions and bake 5 minutes or until onions are golden.

Makes 8 servings

VARIATION: For added Cheddar flavor, substitute **French's®** **Cheddar French Fried Onions** for the original flavor.

INDEX

ACKNOWLEDGMENTS

The publisher would like to thank the companies and organizations listed below for the use of their recipes and photographs in this publication.

Campbell Soup Company

Del Monte Foods

Ortega®, A Division of B&G Foods North America, Inc.

Reckitt Benckiser LLC

Recipes courtesy of the Reynolds Kitchens

Sargento® Foods Inc.

Unilever

Veg•All®

METRIC CONVERSION CHART

VOLUME MEASUREMENTS (dry)

1/8 teaspoon = 0.5 mL
1/4 teaspoon = 1 mL
1/2 teaspoon = 2 mL
3/4 teaspoon = 4 mL
1 teaspoon = 5 mL
1 tablespoon = 15 mL
2 tablespoons = 30 mL
1/4 cup = 60 mL
1/3 cup = 75 mL
1/2 cup = 125 mL
2/3 cup = 150 mL
3/4 cup = 175 mL
1 cup = 250 mL
2 cups = 1 pint = 500 mL
3 cups = 750 mL
4 cups = 1 quart = 1 L

VOLUME MEASUREMENTS (fluid)

1 fluid ounce (2 tablespoons) = 30 mL
4 fluid ounces (1/2 cup) = 125 mL
8 fluid ounces (1 cup) = 250 mL
12 fluid ounces (1 1/2 cups) = 375 mL
16 fluid ounces (2 cups) = 500 mL

WEIGHTS (mass)

1/2 ounce = 15 g
1 ounce = 30 g
3 ounces = 90 g
4 ounces = 120 g
8 ounces = 225 g
10 ounces = 285 g
12 ounces = 360 g
16 ounces = 1 pound = 450 g

DIMENSIONS

1/16 inch = 2 mm
1/8 inch = 3 mm
1/4 inch = 6 mm
1/2 inch = 1.5 cm
3/4 inch = 2 cm
1 inch = 2.5 cm

OVEN TEMPERATURES

250°F = 120°C
275°F = 140°C
300°F = 150°C
325°F = 160°C
350°F = 180°C
375°F = 190°C
400°F = 200°C
425°F = 220°C
450°F = 230°C

BAKING PAN SIZES

Utensil	Size in Inches/Quarts	Metric Volume	Size in Centimeters
Baking or Cake Pan (square or rectangular)	8×8×2	2 L	20×20×5
	9×9×2	2.5 L	23×23×5
	12×8×2	3 L	30×20×5
	13×9×2	3.5 L	33×23×5
Loaf Pan	8×4×3	1.5 L	20×10×7
	9×5×3	2 L	23×13×7
Round Layer Cake Pan	8×1½	1.2 L	20×4
	9×1½	1.5 L	23×4
Pie Plate	8×1¼	750 mL	20×3
	9×1¼	1 L	23×3
Baking Dish or Casserole	1 quart	1 L	—
	1½ quart	1.5 L	—
	2 quart	2 L	—